P9-DOH-217

Good Things TO REMEMBER

MICHAEL PHILLIPS

333 Wise Maxims You Don't Want to Forget

All scripture quotations, unless indicated, are taken from the HOLY BIBLE, NEW INTERNATIONAL VERSION®. Copyright © 1973, 1978, 1984 by International Bible Society. Used by permission of Zondervan Publishing House. All rights reserved. "NIV" and "New International Version" trademarks are registered in the United States Patent and Trademark Office by International Bible Society. Use of either trademark requires the permission of International Bible Society

Copyright © 1993
Michael Phillips
All Rights Reserved

Published by Bethany House Publishers
A Ministry of Bethany Fellowship, Inc.
6820 Auto Club Road, Minneapolis, Minnesota 55438

Printed in the United States of America

ISBN 1–55661–337–7
CIP 92–83967

To MY GOOD FRIEND *Mrs. Heaton*

PRESENTED BY *Michael Peoples*

DATE *June 15, 2000*

Introduction

This may look like a simple little book when you pick it up and flip through it.

Compiling it, however, was anything but simple. When I began reflecting on what a book of "Good Things to Remember" should contain, I found myself drawing from my own Christian walk, sharing principles that were significant to me and quotes from authors who had played a role in my personal development.

The process almost began to take on the feel of a spiritual autobiography as I relived two-and-a-half decades of life with God. It wasn't just a light-hearted jog down memory lane, but a deep encounter—all over again—with men and books and ideas and thoughts that had been a major part of the Lord's work in my heart through the years. I had to interrupt my writing more than once and go to my knees.

On the occasion of reading a certain passage by Henry Drummond, I found myself unexpectedly praying for a particularly difficult superior I had strenuously tried to love some 26 years ago when working in a pulp mill. I had written out Drummond's words on 3×5 cards, taken them to work, and there attempted the practice of the attributes of 1 Corinthians 13 as he details them. My superior happened to be the stone in the middle of my own personal road called Love. Reading Drummond's words once more—there suddenly was his face. Instantly I was back in that hot, grimy, loud boiler room with my 3×5 cards. I took a moment to lift him up in prayer, just as I had done back then with such difficulty.

That's only one of a hundred little stories I could tell you about what this compilation has entailed. The authors I quote, with a few of my own words sprinkled in—this is *my* life . . . these individuals have contributed to all I am as a man. Between the lines flows at least a portion of a life lived with God. I feel I understand some of what William Barclay wrote as he began his autobiography: "It is a good time to look back across life and to ask what the things are by which I have lived."

I have drawn together only what I view as the most essential perspectives by which I *personally* have tried to order my life. In so doing I have tried to keep the thoughts accompanying the quotes brief, but it's difficult not to write several pages (or a whole book) on each one! These are not just sayings I have memorized and stuck up on my wall (though these men's books do occupy a place of honor on my desk). They have gotten inside me and become intrinsic to the sustenance of my being.

This is not to say that every one of the 333 quotes signifies a great crossroads experience, or that every quote symbolizes a huge turning point. Shakespeare's words about music, Thomas Jefferson's about luck, and Andrew Jackson's about courage are all quotes I have come across recently. I find they contain elements of what I value in life; they are principles I want to pass along, especially to my own sons. I find them equally worth heeding, therefore, as the words from Laubach and Kelly and Lewis and MacDonald, which have been with me for twenty years.

How do I know these are "good things" to remember? Because I can specifically testify to the great difference these principles have made to me as I have walked with my Father. If they have value for you on that basis, then I invite you to share my pilgrimage along the path of faith in this way.

I hope a few of these quotes will do the same for you as well.

—Michael Phillips

Bestselling author and novelist Michael Phillips has produced more than fifty books on a wide range of topics. If you find yourself challenged by some of his thoughts in *Good Things To Remember* may we suggest you contact your favorite Christian bookstore or write to Bethany House Publishers for a complete list of titles available by this versatile author. Phillips lives in Eureka, California, with his wife, Judy, and three sons—Patrick, Robin, and Gregory.

Dedication

To the men whom the Father has employed as mentors in my life . . . men whose lives and words and books and example have instilled within me the "good things" of God which I purpose to make it the business of my life to live by and "remember."

The Men

Denver Phillips—who showed me fatherhood and set the example early of a life well-lived in the principles of God, the greatest kind of mentor it is possible to have.

Sam Kleinsasser—a mentor of my childhood, who introduced me to Frank Laubach.

Bill Ellis—a mentor of my youth, who introduced me to Thomas Kelly.

Harold Jackson—a mentor of my young adulthood.

The Authors

Henry Drummond—the mentor of love
C. S. Lewis—the mentor of imaginative reason
Thomas Kelly—the mentor of life at "the Center"
William Barclay—the mentor of love for Scripture
James Dobson—the mentor of multi-generational vision
Francis Schaeffer—the mentor of logic and consistency
Frank Laubach—the mentor of the great "experiment"
George MacDonald—the mentor of Fatherhood and truth

1. *Robert Burns* ▸ I like to have quotations ready for every occasion—they give one's ideas so pat [suitable a form], and save one the trouble of finding expression adequate to one's feelings.

2. Always keep good books around you. Read them—don't let them be mere dust-gatherers.

3. When an author's words get into you, write them down. Keep a file of favorite quotations, with notes of your own thoughts and reminders of what influence you felt at the time of first reading. It is encouraging to be able to look back at various signposts along your own life's journey.

4. *C. S. Lewis* ▸ You find out the strength of a wind by trying to walk against it, not by lying down.

5. Dare to be different. Swim against the world's tide. Go the other direction.

6. *George MacDonald* ▸ Do the truth and you will love the truth.

7. Be clear-minded, thoughtful, applying yourself to understand things. It's Jesus' eighth most frequently given command.

8. Carry proper guilt for things that belong on your shoulders, not false guilt for things that don't. Confess your faults and get them dealt with so you don't have to carry *any*.

9. *Frank Laubach* ▸ Every person we ever meet is God's opportunity.

10. A simple smile and kind word can have an outgoing ripple effect that literally could impact thousands. How many strangers do I just brush thoughtlessly by? Oh, God, open my eyes to them! Yet with every failure, there is renewed challenge. I mustn't let the difficulty obscure the imperative necessity.

11. *Thomas Kelly* ▸ No average goodness will do, no measuring of our lives by our fellows, but only a relentless, inexorable divine standard. No relatives suffice; only absolutes satisfy the soul committed to holy obedience.

12. One of the great signs of maturity is the willingness to readily take "account" for your own mistakes and blunders. Immaturity always tries to shift blame. Maturity shoulders it squarely. Nehemiah and Ezra understood this principle, and I love them for their example. "In all that has happened . . . we did wrong . . . we assume the responsibility . . ." (Nehemiah 9:33; 10:32).

13. Keep clear in your mind the enormous distinction between truth and opinion. Everyone has a vast supply of personal ideas and preferences and half-baked viewpoints. We're told, however, to live by *truth,* which is an altogether different thing and is rooted in God's commands, laws, and decrees. *Truth* is what we're to pass to our children and those around us, not just a list of our own personal affinities and predilections. Know which is coming out of your mouth when you speak.

14. *George MacDonald* ▸ What is called a good conscience is often but a dull one that gives no trouble when it ought to bark the loudest.

15. Keep open-minded in both directions. Open yourself to truth contained in the opinions you *don't* hold, and to falsehoods inherent in the opinions you *do* hold. All "opinion" contains elements of both truth *and* error. Only with a double-directional open-mindedness will you arrive at the center point of balanced *truth*.

16. *C. S. Lewis* ▸ He warned people to "count the cost" before becoming Christians. "Make no mistake," He says, "if you let me, I will make you perfect. The moment you put yourself in My hands, that is what you are in for. Nothing less. I will never rest, nor let you rest, until My Father can say without reservation that He is well-pleased with you. This I can do and will do. But I will not do anything less."

17. A lot of our evangelism is get-'em-saved-and-worry-about-the-rest-later. Such wasn't Jesus' way. He got the cost-counting on the table, and let people walk away if they weren't prepared to go the distance.

18. *Thomas Kelly* ▸ Deep within us all there is an amazing inner sanctuary of the soul, a holy place, a Divine Center, a speaking Voice, to which we may continuously return. Eternity is at our hearts, pressing upon our time-torn lives, warming us with intimations of an astounding destiny, calling us home unto Itself. Yielding to these persuasions, gladly committing ourselves in body and soul, utterly and completely, to the Light Within, is the beginning of true life.

19. The real business of life is inside—where we think and
feel and choose. That is the *real* world, not the outside
busy place where our hands and feet do their business.
Are you really alive? Are you living in the inner or outer
world? Are you familiar with life in the "Center," or are
you a stranger there? I must confess that, though I am
well acquainted with that country, I do not spend as much
time there as I long to. I'm not a stranger, though I would
still have to consider myself a "visitor." Kelly first
introduced me to the region, and I'm praying daily to get
more and more pieces of my life moved there so I can
begin to consider myself a permanent resident.

20. *George MacDonald* ▸ The business of life is not to get as much as you can, but to do justly, and love mercy, and walk humbly with your God.

21. Make sure your books have smudges on them from heavy use—your use and other people's. A perfectly clean, unsoiled book is like a car with a zero odometer reading— nice to look at, but it hasn't been anywhere.

22. Pray daily: Lord, show me what you want me to say. Help me say it.

23. *George MacDonald* ▸ The beautiful things around us are the expressions of God's face.

24. The incredible truth of Romans 1:20–21 is that we really *can* get to know a lot about God from the world and the people He has made. To observe the world is like stepping into God's private office and examining everything in it to discover what we can learn about Him. God created everything for that purpose—to reveal His personality and character.

25. Discover the difference between righteous anger and selfish anger. The former is an attribute of God, the latter is a sin we must rid from our hearts. When anger erupts because the *self* has been crossed, it's of the flesh. There's nothing good about it!

26. *Henry Drummond* ▸ Paul passes this thing, Love, through the magnificent prism of his inspired intellect, and it comes out on the other side broken up into its elements. And in these few words we have what one might call the Spectrum of Love, the analysis of Love. Will you notice what its elements are? Will you notice that they have common names; that they are virtues which we hear about every day; that they are things which can be practiced by every man in every place in life; and how, by a multitude of small things and ordinary virtues, the supreme thing, the *summum bonum,* is made up.

27. When the biblical writers give instructions about what we are to do, all of them are extremely practical and down-to-earth. Where does all our theorizing come from? So much of the Scriptures, as Drummond says, have to do with "things which can be practiced by every man in every place in life."

28. The fruit of the Spirit in Galatians 5 are so incredibly *do-able!* The very familiarity of the words tends to obscure how astoundingly simple they really are—love, joy, peace, patience, kindness, goodness, faithfulness, gentleness, self-control. Love has nine attributes. The fruit of the spiritual life is revealed in these nine ways. Is there anything else in all the world to make the goal of life! Aren't these characteristics the very essence of wisdom and a Christlike existence?

29. *George MacDonald* ▸ To open us to its infinite unseen world, love is teaching us to love all men, and live for all men.

30. *Mr. Fred Rogers* ▸ You always make each day special. You know how—just by being you!

31. Made in the image of God, how could it be otherwise? There are huge caverns of wonderful goodness within every individual you meet. True, it may be encrusted over from years of forgetfulness, but still it awaits discovery anew. See if you can find the doorway into that cavern inside the next person you encounter.

32. Fiction was one of Jesus' most often-used methods of conveying truth. The novels of George MacDonald are the most *real* of all the books I have encountered in my life. They have infused more of the principles of God than all the didactic, "teaching" books on my shelves put together. Seek out good, solid fiction as a beneficial and nutritional component of your literary diet. Read them to *discover* life, not to escape from it.

33. *Soren Kierkegaard* ▸ The first requirement is that you must not look at the mirror and inspect the mirror but see yourself in the mirror. . . . The witness of truth warns against the error of coming to inspect the mirror instead of to see oneself in the mirror. . . . God's Word is the mirror. By reading or hearing it I shall see myself in the mirror.

For Self-Examination

34. Why is it a "good thing" to *remember*? The word *remember* is used approximately 154 times in the Bible. More of those are found in Deuteronomy than any book other than the Psalms. That's not by accident. There's a good reason. Moses was on to something. We are supposed to *remind* ourselves of the commands, decrees, and laws of God. We are supposed to think of them, talk about them, and *remember* them. We are to "fix them" in our minds. We are to write them, talk about them, discuss them, and "impress" them upon our hearts. We are supposed to *REMEMBER* the things of God.

35. *George MacDonald* ▸ Everything has a soul and a body, or something like them. By the body we know the soul. But we are always ready to love the body instead of the soul. Therefore, God makes the body die continually, that we may learn to love the soul indeed.

36. *George MacDonald* ▸ There exists a mystery in the world, and in all the looks of it—a mystery because of a meaning. There is a jubilance in every sunrise, a sober sadness in every sunset. There is a whispering of strange secrets in the wind of the twilight, and an unknown bliss in the song of the lark.

37. Give people the benefit of the doubt. That's what "rejoices with the truth" means. When someone says something that hurts, choose to interpret it non-hurtfully. Put the best, most positive, most gracious construction on their comment you can think of. If there's no way to keep it from hurting, then immediately summon forgiveness to the rescue. Otherwise a wall's going to go up between you and the other—and *you* will have been the one to build it.

38. *Henry Drummond* ▸ The Spectrum of Love has nine ingredients . . . Patience; kindness; generosity; humility; courtesy; unselfishness; good temper; guilelessness; sincerity—these make up the supreme gift, the stature of the perfect man. You will observe that all are in relation to men, in relation to life, in relation to the known to-day and the near to-morrow, and not to the unknown eternity . . . The supreme thing, in short, is not a thing at all, but the giving of a further finish to the multitudinous words and acts which make up the sum of every common day.

39. Jesus spent most of His life *doing,* not philosophizing—doing, believe it or not, what we might term "unspiritual" things. Is He our example? Then we must love! How? By *doing* the nine things Paul wrote about in 1 Corinthians 13:4–8.

40. Ask, "Lord, what would you do here?" several times a day.

41. Successful people operate in an environment where success is the norm. They expect things to be done right because they place that expectation upon *themselves.* The environment of success, order, efficiency, and productivity is self-imposed. It happens also to be the way our Father functions.

42. *Thomas Kelly* ▸ Between the relinquished past and the untrodden future stands the holy Now, whose bulk has swelled to cosmic size, for within the Now is the dwelling place of God himself. In the Now we are home at last.

43. There is nothing else we have but the present, the NOW. It is the great gift of God, the great opportunity of the ages! There is nothing else.

44. Don't wait. If you put off "living" for some other moment than the present five minutes, Life will always elude you, for life is made up of an endless succession of *nows*.

45. *C. S. Lewis* ▸ I think we must admit that the discussion of disputed points has no tendency at all to bring an outsider into the Christian fold. So long as we write and talk about them we are much more likely to deter him from entering any Christian communion.

46. All your life long, resist with absolute determination the deadening and unscriptural proclivity to turn the "true spirituality" that Jesus lived and taught into a matter of ideas and doctrines and discussion. This tendency pervades *every* church bearing His name in all the world. Don't let it snare you and lull you into a spiritual stupor. Keep your spiritual focus awake!

47. *Francis Schaeffer* ▶ Through the centuries men have displayed many different symbols to show that they are Christians. They have worn marks in the lapels of their coats, hung chains about their necks, even had special haircuts.

Of course, there is nothing intrinsically wrong with any of this, if one feels it is his calling. But there is a much better sign— . . . a universal mark that is to last through all the ages of the church until Jesus comes back. . . .

Love—and the unity it attests to—is the mark Christ gave Christians to *wear* before the world. Only with this mark may the world know that Christians are indeed Christians and that Jesus was sent by the Father.

The Mark of the Christian

48. There is an enormous misconception pervading all of society, all of religion, all of culture, that Truth can be conveyed and transmitted by words alone. "Information" may be implanted in the brain by words. But the kind of *truth* that men and women *live* is a matter of the heart. Things don't get inside the heart where life is changed without *seeing* truth as well as hearing it.

49. Live and teach your family to consider yourselves part of the larger body of God's people. Our time on earth is designed to train us in readiness for spending eternity among the community of the saints.

50. *George MacDonald* ▸ Nature's so-called laws are the waving of God's garments, waving so because he is thinking and loving and walking inside them.

51. The egg, the acorn, the trunk of a tree, the symmetry and order of the natural universe, and the human heart . . . none are merely what they appear on the outside. Everything has a yoke and a shell, a husk and a seed, a trunk outside the sap, a body and soul. Train your eyes to look inside. To find *life* you have to probe deeper.

52. *Jesus Christ* ▸ By this all men will know that you are my disciples, if you love one another.   John 13:35

53. We may be able to "tell" someone what we believe—the *ideas* of our intellectual belief system—in a vacuum. But if we want them to know that we are really Christ's disciples, that His life means everything to us, that we live by it and would die for it, and that we would serve them as a result—there is only one way to convey all *that*. Jesus told us how to transmit our *discipleship* to others in John 13:35.

54. *Francis Schaeffer* ▸ Jesus is giving a right to the world. Upon His authority He gives the world the right to judge whether you and I are born-again Christians on the basis of our observable love toward all Christians. *The Mark of the Christian*

55. *Jesus Christ* ▸ My prayer is not for them alone. I pray also for those who will believe in me through their message, that all of them may be one, Father, just as you are in me and I am in you. . . . May they be brought to complete unity to let the world know that you sent me and have loved them even as you have loved me. John 17:20–21, 23

56. Is it conceivable that a prayer of Christ's will go unanswered? I think not. Therefore, we may conclude that unity will happen between His people and that the world *will* one day know that the Father sent Him.

57. Go through the Psalms, Proverbs, and books of the New Testament and list every direct command that applies to you. Make this a lifetime study. Then *do* them.

58. *C. S. Lewis* ▸ Fine feelings, new insights, greater interest in "religion" mean nothing unless they make our actual behaviour better . . . the outer world is quite right to judge Christianity by its results. Christ told us to judge by results. A tree is known by its fruit. . . . When we Christians behave badly, or fail to behave well, we are making Christianity unbelievable to the outside world . . . we give them grounds . . . that throws doubt on the truth of Christianity itself.

59. Give God thanks for *exactly* how He put your body and mind together. He knew what He was doing! There is no one just like you!

60. You don't have to have the "best," even when you can afford it. Voluntary self-denial is a healthy and maturing factor to make a regular part of your life.

61. *C. S. Lewis* ▸ The principle runs through all life from top to bottom. Give up your self, and you will find your real self. Lose your life and you will save it. Submit to death, death of your ambitions and favourite wishes every day . . . submit with every fibre of your being, and you will find eternal life. Keep nothing back. Nothing that you have not given away will ever be really yours . . . look for Christ and you will find Him, and with Him everything else thrown in.

62. We esteem others with more than mere words, but also by gestures, looks, and body language. By subtleties and innuendoes innumerable (usually that we are unaware of), we build people up or make them feel small.

63. Remember why God gave the Law—to bring order and purpose to life, to guide people into loving and unselfish relationships, and to infuse His character into their daily actions and attitudes.

64. Get to know the characters in George MacDonald's novels. Consider them friends and role models. If you don't yet know Malcolm, Robert Falconer, Mary Marston, wee Sir Gibbie, Donal Grant, Hugh Sutherland, Annie Anderson, Thomas Wingfold, and Joseph Polwarth personally, you are in for some adventures and growth in relationship!

65. *C. S. Lewis* ▸ I find a good many people bothered by . . . Our Lord's words, "Be ye perfect." Some people seem to think this means "Unless you are perfect, I will not help you"; and as we cannot be perfect, then . . . our position is hopeless. But I do not think He did mean that. I think He meant "The only help I will give is help to become perfect. You may want something less: but I will give you nothing less."

66. What God calls us to is not a perfectionism of result. That we will fail and fall short all our lives is a given. Ongoing forgiveness (seventy times seven) is intrinsic to the equation. He calls us rather to perfection of "motive" and of "end result." He wants us to *want* to obey Him perfectly, so that *in the end* we will be made like Jesus. That's what the command, "Be perfect," means.

67. Remain vigilant and alert. It's Jesus' third most frequently given command, far more emphasized than many commands that seem at first glance to be more "spiritual."

68. You don't learn from voicing your own opinions.

69. *George MacDonald* ▸ Of course no one can perfectly keep a single commandment. . . . And there is no keeping of them other than a perfect keeping. To keep them means to keep them perfectly. But though I hold with all my heart that no keeping of the commandments but a perfect one will satisfy God, it is not true that there is no other kind he cares for. He will not be satisfied with less, yet he will be delighted with all honest movements, however small, in that direction. What father is not pleased with the first tottering attempt of his little one to walk? Yet at the same time, what father would be satisfied with anything but the manly step of the full-grown son?

70. An intrinsic difference exists between being a *believer* and being a *disciple*. A person may be both, yet it is possible to be only the former and not the latter.

71. When we choose to want something *less* than what God ultimately has designed for us, letting ourselves off the hook for halfheartedness of obedience to His instructions because, after all, "We're only human . . . what do you expect anyway . . . nobody's perfect"; then we are not walking as one of His disciples. It is possible to make this justification for a tepid and apathetic approach to faith and still be a "believer." But such a one is *not* walking as a disciple.

72. *C. S. Lewis* ▸ We say, "I never expected to be a saint, I only wanted to be a decent ordinary chap." And we imagine when we say this that we are being humble. But this is the fatal mistake. Of course we never wanted and never asked to be made into the sort of creatures He is going to make us into. But the question is not what we intended ourselves to be, but what He intended us to be when He made us. . . . We may be content to remain what we call "ordinary people": but He is determined to carry out a quite different plan. To shrink back from that plan is not humility; it is laziness and cowardice. To submit to it . . . is obedience.

73. Remember that no one denomination or Christian organization or system of truth has a corner on the truth—even yours . . . and mine!

74. *Andrew Jackson* ▸ One man with courage makes a majority.

75. *Apostle Paul* ▸ Be strong in the Lord. . . . Put on the full armor of God. . . . Stand your ground. . . . After you have done everything, to stand. Stand firm.   *Ephesians 6:10–14*

76. *Anonymous* ▸ The present circumstance which presses so hard against you, if surrendered to Jesus, is the best shaped tool in the Master's hand to chisel you for eternity. Trust Him then, do not push away the instrument, lest you spoil the work.

77. The piercing truths in the forty preceding anonymous
words have shown a mirror to my own self-motives and
untrusting nature more times than any other single quote
or passage of scripture. They quite literally have changed
my whole outlook on the nature of God's work in human
life. These brief words have been molding and shaping my
character and outlook on *everything* for more than thirty
years. If you let them inside, I promise an odyssey in the
discovery of God's work in *your* heart!

78. Explore ways to structure and arrange and organize the affairs of your life so that you reach your objectives but are as independent from the world's systems as possible. Not to be isolationist, but rather, as Oswald Chambers calls it, "fundamentally disconnected."

79. Help people when they genuinely need it. But allow them to learn from their own mistakes rather than shielding them from them. Be prudent when you are called upon to bail someone out who is likely to jump right back into the same fix again.

80. *Henry Drummond* ▸ If a man does not exercise his soul, he acquires no muscle in his soul, no strength of character, no vigor of moral fibre, nor beauty of spiritual growth. Love is not a thing of enthusiastic emotion. It is a rich, strong, manly, vigorous expression of the whole round Christian character—the Christlike nature in its fullest development. And the constituents of this great character are only to be built up by ceaseless practice.

81. Don't step between a person's foolish action and the natural consequences of that action. In so doing, you prevent one of life's most effective teachers from being able to do its maturing work.

82. Accountability is one of the most missing elements of truth in all of today's society. When allowed to do its work, it is powerful for the practical implantation of truth. Though the rest of the world is moving in directions that may result in the word *accountability* being stricken from its vocabulary, don't *you* lose sight of its absolutely imperative importance. Most of all with respect to *yourself*!

83. Maturity begins with accountability. Taking "account" is one of the chief methods for "exercising" the muscles of character. It's impossible to grow strong in integrity without this quality deeply infused into one's being.

84. *Richard Foster* ▸ Our world is hungry for genuinely changed people.   *Celebration of Discipline*

85. Consider the logical consequences of your thoughts: If followed to its logical extension, what implications does this seemingly simple idea have in my life and in the lives of others.

86. *C. S. Lewis* ▸ The terrible thing, the almost impossible thing, is to hand over your whole self . . . to Christ. But it is far easier than what we are all trying to do instead. For what we are trying to do is to remain what we call "ourselves," to keep personal happiness as our great aim in life, and yet at the same time be "good." We are all trying to let our mind and heart go their own way . . . and hoping, in spite of this, to behave honestly and chastely and humbly. And that is exactly what Christ warned us you could not do. A thistle cannot produce figs. If I am a field that contains nothing but grass seed, I cannot produce wheat. Cutting the grass may keep it short: but I shall still produce grass and no wheat. If I want to produce wheat, the change must go deeper than the suface. I must be plowed up and resown.

87. God is in the business of transformation, not the establishment of a worldwide religious organization. Transformation happens one person, one word, one kind gesture, one forgiving smile, one thought, one attitude at a time. He is making us into new creatures, into people of a certain sort, into men and women who reflect the very character of His Son.

88. Always an appropriate prayer: Slow me down, Lord.

89. Eternity reduces to the present, the immediate, the now.

90. *Cary Grant* ▸ The only people who grow old were born old to begin with. If you're young, you'll remain that way. *The Bishop's Wife*

91. Don't pass by life's joys. Jesus not only wept, He knew how to laugh.

92. *C. S. Lewis* ▸ What God cares about is not exactly our actions. What He cares about is that we should be creatures of a certain kind or quality—the kind of creatures He intended us to be—creatures related to Himself in a certain way.

93. *C. S. Lewis* ▸ Good and evil both increase at compound interest. That is why the little decisions you and I make every day are of such infinite importance. The smallest good act today is the capture of a strategic point from which, a few months later, you may be able to go on to victories you never dreamed of. An apparently trivial indulgence in lust or anger today is the loss of a ridge or railway line or bridgehead from which the enemy may launch an attack otherwise impossible.

94. The entire Christian reduces to what you do, say, and think, the attitudes you hold, and the choices you make in the next five minutes. The course of your life is determined by the three hundred seconds immediately in front of you, and what use you choose to make of them.

95. There are four essential steps by which truth is implanted into our being: seeking information, making mental application, making practical application, applying learned principles in our lives. If one is left out, truth will be incomplete. The final step is the most important.

96. *George MacDonald* ▸ He regards men not as they are merely, but as they shall be; not as they shall be merely, but as they are now growing, or capable of growing, toward that image after which he made them that they might grow to it. Therefore a thousand stages, each in itself all but valueless, are of inestimable worth as the necessary and connected gradations of an infinite progress. A condition which of declension would indicate a devil, may of growth indicate a saint.

97. The surface appearance of an interaction reveals very little about two individuals who may be involved. What determines everything is this: What direction is each moving internally?

98. Two people meet at some place on the "scale of inner selflessness." One is moving toward the *light of selflessness;* the other moves toward the *darkness of selfishness.* Their passage is but a momentary intersection of apparent sameness. In reality, the two are as different as night and day, as the years will reveal. The darkness will increasingly engulf the one; radiance will steadily shine out of the other.

99. *George MacDonald* ▸ Two people may be at the same spot in manners and behaviour, and yet one may be getting better and the other worse, which is the greatest of all differences that could possibly exist between them.

100. No man can determine in which direction another is moving, toward or away from the Light. Every individual holds in his hand only the power to determine his *own* direction and destiny.

101. Find new beauty in the things you pass every day.

102. Pray daily: Lord, show me who I am. Help me to walk in it.

103. Voice concerns in a positive, gracious, non-accusatory manner.

104. You are unlikely to change your spouse. Remembering this will save you both much grief. (Don't ask either my wife or me to explain further!)

105. Go beyond the surface. Life and consequences both originate in the subsoil where roots gain their nourishment.

106. *C. S. Lewis* ▸ God is to be obeyed because of what He is in Himself. If you ask why we should obey God, in the last resort the answer is, "I am."
Surprised by Joy

107. The great curse of modernism has infected the Church with lethal but unseen injections of humanism. Even the message of God's love that we take to the world is shaped from a humanistic viewpoint, beginning with all God will do *for us*. It is all backward. Everything must originate with who God is. "In the beginning God . . ."

108. Our motive for coming to God should not be for blessings, for experiences, to have our "life changed," because He answers our prayers, because He will fill us with joy and purpose, nor even because He forgives our sin. *Our* life has nothing to do with the fundamental issue of the universe. Obedience is required, at the rock-bottom foundation, by virtue of who God is. Nothing else. God is God. "I am." Out of that *I-Am-ness* flows His life and all it means. But it must be in that order.

109. Flowers grow everywhere. Wherever you are, whatever you are doing, however fast you may sometimes have to move . . . stop to smell them. They are a visible, beautiful link from our hectic world right into God's heart.

110. Know your spiritual mentors. Give them credit often for who you are.

111. *Oswald Chambers* ▸ I am reading George MacDonald's *There and Back*. Of course MacDonald appeals to my bias. I love that writer.

Oswald Chambers, His Life and Work

112. *C. S. Lewis* ▸ In MacDonald it is always the voice of conscience that speaks. He addresses the will: the demand for obedience, for "something to be neither more nor less nor other than *done*" is incessant. . . . In making this collection I was discharging a debt of justice. I have never concealed the fact that I regarded him as my master; indeed I fancy I have never written a book in which I did not quote from him. . . . Honesty drives me to emphasise it . . . I dare not say that he is never in error; but to speak plainly I know hardly any other writer who seems to be closer, or more continually close, to the Spirit of Christ Himself.

George MacDonald, An Anthology

113. Chamber's and Lewis's words of affection for George
MacDonald are included here because of the importance
of paying tribute to those who have helped make us what
we are. Maturity is not arrived at all at once. Truth is
implanted and spread through the world
multigenerationally. Lewis and Chambers, so influential in
the twentieth century, owed many of their spiritual roots
to MacDonald's work in the nineteenth. And they said so.
It's the very pattern observed throughout the Old
Testament and commanded by God. This is an intrinsic
aspect of the "remembering" injunction given us by
Moses in Deuteronomy.

114. *Thomas Jefferson* ▸ I am a great believer in luck. The harder I work, the more I have of it.

115. The purpose of the Bible is to reveal who God is. It keeps every page of God's Word so fresh for me to know that at any moment—unexpectedly . . . wonderfully . . . a nugget of gold suddenly shining up from under a rock!—I may discover some new facet of His personality that I didn't fully appreciate before.

116. *Continuation* is the key to following the commands of Deuteronomy 6:1–9. My sons and I go out on every one of our birthdays for a "birthday walk" to talk about just this single truth.

117. Learn to blend analysis and emotions, mind and heart. Don't give way to either to the exclusion of the other.

118. *George MacDonald* ▸ Lord, let me ever and aye see thy face, and desire nothing more—except that the whole world, O Lord, may behold it likewise.

119. Every atom of life is a revelation of God.

120. *George MacDonald* ▸ It is on them that do His will that the day dawns. To them the Daystar rises in their hearts. Obedience is the soul of knowledge.

121. The sensitivity to read people, to feel sympathy with their emotions and mood and insecurities and thoughts, is a learned art you can develop.

122. *George MacDonald* ▸ How much the coming of the kingdom is retarded by an absence of courtesy.

123. Courtesy and sensitivity are born in servanthood and express themselves in a gracious, tender, compassionate spirit.

124. *George MacDonald* ▸ Upon obedience must our energy be spent; understanding will follow.

125. Everything originates with God. He is the initiator. I can only respond. In prayer, in decisions, in actions and attitudes, the Lord breathes life into all I do and say and think. I return my part in this divinely harmonious relationship in obedience and in faithfulness to the principles He has established for me to follow.

126. *C. S. Lewis* ▸ If once we allow people to start spiritualizing and refining, or as they might say, "deepening," the sense of the word *Christian,* it will speedily become a useless word.

127. "Spiritual" has to do with the world of the *spirit* rather than the physical, temporal, material "world." It is in the kingdom of the spirit where God's principles and truths operate, unseen by "worldly" eyes. Acquiring a truly spiritual outlook and frame of reference takes years and years of walking in obedience to the commands, truths, priorities, perspectives, and instructions of God.

128. To "spiritualize" is an attempt to take something from the physical, material world and turn it into a *spiritual* thing by applying spiritual-sounding words to it. But there are no shortcuts to true spirituality.

129. Consider yourself "a part" of more than one church in your area. Not only will it keep your view of God's body expansive, you will be enriched by the diversity of relationships.

130. *Leo Tolstoy* ► Everybody thinks of changing humanity and nobody thinks of changing himself.

131. The down-to-earth principles outlined in the book of Proverbs are life's most practical guidebook. The Christian wanting to live in integrity, and anyone who wants his life to be a success by any standard, will find every principle there by which to live and reach his goals.

132. *Miles Stanford* ▸ There are no shortcuts to reality! . . . there is always danger of turning to the false enticement of a shortcut via the means of "experiences," and "blessings," where one becomes pathetically enmeshed in the vortex of ever-changing "feelings," adrift from the moorings of scriptural facts.

133. Laying a pious gloss on top of the ordinary occurrences of life will not take the maturing place of years, nor cause spirituality to emerge before its time. Therefore, don't "spiritualize" what doesn't belong to the spirit. You can't fake Christlikeness.

134. *George MacDonald* ▸ It is a most dangerous thing to use sacred words often. It makes them so common to our ear that at length, when used most solemnly, they have not half the effect they ought to have, and that is a serious loss.

135. Keep truth close. Arm's-length spirituality is not what Jesus died for.

136. *George MacDonald* ▸ Man's first business is, "What does God want me to do?"

137. It is fearfully easy to engage in the process of externalizing deep truths, getting them as far away from the unpleasant and uncomfortable region of the heart, and out into our hands, where we can DO something instead of BE a certain kind of person.

138. *Frank Laubach* ▸ It is a moment-by-moment, every waking moment, surrender, responsiveness, obedience, sensitivity, pliability, lostness in His love, that I now have the mind-bent to explore with all my might. It means two burning passions: First, to be like Jesus. Second, to respond to God as a violin responds to the bow of the master.

139. The prayer to be made like Jesus carries a huge price tag. If you pray it, mean it down to the very depths, because God desires nothing more than to answer it. Count the cost! This is one of those principles I mentioned in the Introduction that I could write a whole book about. Nearly every chapter would involve pain. And tears. The life to which He calls us is not an easy one.

140. Christlikeness is the only goal of the human race.

141. Find plenty of opportunities *every* day to sincerely apologize.

142. Find *lots* of opportunities every day to express gratitude. Do it with a smile!

143. *George MacDonald* ▸ Obedience is the opener of eyes.

144. Memorize Scripture.

145. DO what the scriptures you've memorized tell you. Don't learn verses you don't know how or intend to apply.

146. *George MacDonald* ▸ Fatherhood is the last height of the human stair whence our understanding can see God afar off.

147. That God is our Father is THE central truth of the universe. The universe literally hangs together by this truth.

148. God's Fatherhood was the singular focal point of Jesus' mission on earth. It was the reason He could work miracles, the reason He died, the reason He rose, the reason He sent His Spirit to dwell in our hearts, and the reason for every work He carries out within us and in the world.

149. *George MacDonald* ▸ To become God's true sons and daughters are we created; it is the one end of our being.

150. Everything that Jesus did was to point us to the Father (and He said so).

151. Don't make the fatal mistake of assuming the fatherhood of your earthly father is an accurate representation of God's. It can't be. It was never intended to carry such a burden. As humans we are imperfect vessels, merely foreshadowing the divine.

152. Earthly parenthood is intended as a picture of God, though a shadowy one, as a "type" of God's Fatherhood.

153. *George MacDonald* ▸ This is and has been the Father's work from the beginning—to bring us into the home of his heart. This is our destiny.

154. *George MacDonald* ▸ Love is the deepest in God, the deepest depth, the essence of his nature, at the root of all his being. Every divine attribute we think to ascribe to him rests upon his love. God's love is what he *is*.

155. *George MacDonald* ▸ God is visible all around us, but only to the man or woman who *would* see him.

156. There are certain large, encompassing, overarching, eternal, and unchanging "General" truths about God and His character, into which a whole range of smaller, temporal, less sweeping "Specific" principles, events, and passages of Scripture must fit. Make sure you don't get it backward and try to shrink the *General* so that you can stuff it into the box marked *specific*.

157. If modification of an interpretation is required, you have to change your view of the *specific*. God's character and being mustn't be devalued in order to make it fit into some specific portion of Scripture that on the surface appears to contradict the *General*. All *specifics* have to be viewed by the light of the *General* truths we are told about God.

158. *Evangelism begins with separation.* To go "into" the world with effectiveness, Christians must first have come "out" of the world. Without a visible *difference*, and a distinct separation, there can be no evangelism.

159. God called Abraham to leave Ur as the basis for revealing himself to all the world. Abraham was the first "evangelist," so to speak. God's purpose of worldwide revelation of himself began with one *man* being called apart, then one *nation* being chosen and called to separate itself from the nations around it, spreading since the time of Jesus to a *people* called to be "holy and peculiar" and "set apart." It's all backward from how we might have done it. But then God's ways usually are.

160. *Oswald Chambers* ▸ We are to be *in* the world but not *of* it; to be disconnected fundamentally, not externally.   *My Utmost for His Highest*

161. In God's kingdom everything is upside down. He says, "Tell the world of me by having nothing to do with the world." He says, "They will heed you only if you do not live like them."

162. Take advice.

163. Ask for recommendations.

164. Take no offense when you are given counsel. If it is wise, follow it.

165. Hunger for input.

166. *George MacDonald* ▸ The good for which we are born into this world is that we may learn to love.

167. A man's or woman's responses to the input of others is one of the things that separates the men from the boys, the women from the girls, the wise men from the fools, the mature from the immature.

168. The person who is hungry and eager for and dedicates himself to seeking well-founded wisdom from others is a growing, learning, mature individual destined himself to become wise and who will discover a wealth of rich relationships along the way.

169. Look for ideas.

170. The man or woman who turns away input from others, who is satisfied within himself and with what he or she already knows and has experienced, is an individual destined for personal stagnation, self-absorption, and pallid, shallow relationships.

171. *George MacDonald* ▸ Foolish is the man, and there are many such men, who would set the world right by waging war on the evils around him, while he neglects that integral part of the world where lies his business, his first business—namely, his own character and conduct.

172. Morality and righteousness will never be imposed by force upon the world. Nor by Christian activism. Jesus said, "My kingdom is not of this world."

173. Details matter.

174. "Freedom in the Spirit" is no license for a random and unplanned life. God's ways are never chaotic, disorganized, or full of confusion.

175. *Miles Stanford* ▸ Today is the day to put our hand to the plow, and irrevocably set our heart on His goal for us.

176. Moving randomly through life, taking just what "comes" and however momentum leads you, is a certain pathway to ineffectiveness, disorganization, and a blurry focus. It is not God's way.

177. *C. S. Lewis* ▸ We have not yet had the slightest
notion of the tremendous thing He means to make of
us. . . . Imagine yourself as a living house. God
comes in to rebuild that house. At first, perhaps,
you can understand what He is doing. He is getting
the drains right and stopping the leaks in the roof
and so on. . . . But presently He starts knocking
the house about in a way that hurts. . . . You
thought you were going to be made into a decent
little cottage: but He is building a palace. He intends
to come and live in it Himself.

178. There will always be within us the inbred, habitual tendency to gravitate toward small specific principles rather than large General truths. The smaller the truth, the easier it is to externalize. Fight it inside yourself tooth and nail!

179. *George MacDonald* ▸ Our business is not to think correctly, but to live truly. Then first will there be a possibility of our thinking correctly.

180. The grace of God is not an escape hatch when things don't go as we'd planned. Grace doesn't excuse foolishness or selfishness or irresponsibility.

181. *C. S. Lewis* ▸ When He said, "Be perfect," He meant it. He meant that we must go in for the full treatment. It is hard; but the sort of compromise we are all hankering after is harder—in fact, it is impossible. It may be hard for an egg to turn into a bird: it would be a jolly sight harder for it to learn to fly while remaining an egg. We are like eggs at present. And you cannot go on indefinitely being just an ordinary, decent egg. We must be hatched or go bad.

182. *Denver Phillips (my dad)* ▸ If your fingers can touch it, you should catch it.

This injunction from my father, which I've passed on to my own sons with the football in our backyard, yields a quick dozen "good things to remember" to last a lifetime:

183. *Reach High!*

184. *If something's worth going after, it's worth getting.*

185. *Make extra effort.*

186. *Make life fun.*

187. *If you have to leave your feet to make the catch, then . . . jump! In other words, there come times in life to take risks—not often, but only when a well-planned "jump" will snag the objective.*

188. *Cherish special moments with those you love.*

189. *Play with your sons and daughters.*

190. *Build memories.*

191. *There are no insignificant moments.*

192. *Infuse principles of truth into your children whenever you have the opportunity.*

193. *YOU are accountable. Don't blame others when things go wrong and you* don't *make the catch.*

194. *When something slips through your fingers, look to yourself. Don't pass the buck. Making the catch depends on no one else but you. Get up and try again!*

195. There are all kinds of hidden levels of meaning to most everything. Find and discover the subsurface meanings and applications to what "seem" like simple statements, situations, and settings. Your life will be enriched, and you will glean ten chunks of wisdom from every apparently "simple" statement or encounter.

196. Be a thinker. Keep your mind active. Energize your brain to hunt for and discover the usually overlooked truths between-the-lines.

197. *George MacDonald* ▸ For everything that God has made, there is layer upon layer of ascending significance.

198. Every man or woman (especially those closest to us!) have volumes to teach us—without their even knowing it—if we are watching and listening with an eager learner's and discoverer's mentality. As Solomon reminded us over and over, wisdom is there for *anyone*, but it must be sought with diligence.

199. Build second- and third-generation Christians. Place high value and work on the spiritual legacy you leave behind for those who follow. Make sure they know what their heritage is from you.

200. *George MacDonald* ▸ Practicality is the code of true faith: can something be *done*? If so, where is to be found the first opportunity to *do* it?

201. *George MacDonald* ▸ Do not be as the fools who think of nothing but Christ as a theological person to be discussed, and do not set themselves to do his words.

202. Anyone can be an *equipper*—one who endows and enables other people with the "equipment" (mostly internal) to fulfill their dreams. You have more tools at your disposal than you probably realize.

203. The training of sons and daughters does not end with their adulthood. It is to be multi-generational. Read Deuteronomy 6:1–9. The process has not just to do with *our* children, but with their children after them. The duty upon us is to build continually into the ongoing generational flow of the nation of God's people. God does not intend for these links to be broken.

204. *George MacDonald* ► Who but a father could think up, call into being, such creations as the flowers for his little ones?

205. *George MacDonald* ► We must not love the outside as if it were the inside. Everything comes that we may know the sender, of whom it is a symbol, a far-off likeness of something in him. And to him it must lead us.

206. Incredible as it seems, there is a certain branch of pietism that talks as if some of the old-fashioned virtues, like *goodness,* are really, according to the Bible, bad things. It puts black above white and the devil above God, makes hell a deeper truth in the economy of eternity than God's victory, and declares the starting point for the gospel to be sin instead of love. Nonsense. God is higher than all blackness.

207. In spite of sin, there is a lot of *good* in the world. God created every molecule to reflect His nature. Goodness is a "good" thing. Jesus spent His lifetime doing "good," and teaching others to do likewise.

208. *George MacDonald* ▸ One of the most unchristian things is to dispute and separate in the name of him whose one object was, and whose one victory will be, unity.

209. God is a God of order, rationality, and logic. We might not always understand everything of God, but His methods—if we could only see far enough into them—do not violate common sense and reason.

210. *Howard Hendricks* ▸ The Christian life is a marathon, not a 100 yard dash.

211. In the things of greatest value, you're not going to see immediate results. Longevity and stick-to-itiveness are basic principles, not just with regard to success in the world, but in the kingdom of God as well.

212. *Frank Laubach* ▸ Tonight, lonesome and half ill with a cold, I am learning from experience that there is a deep peace that grows out of illness and loneliness and a sense of failure. These things do drive me up my hill to God, and then there comes into my soul through the very tears a comfort which is so much better than laughter.

213. We are commanded to come out from among the peoples of the world and be distinctive and separate. Peter calls us "a peculiar people." Paul commands us not to conform to the world's value system. Find out what this means practically in *your* life.

214. Evangelism is not *primarily* a transmission of information. The ineffectiveness of our evangelism exists precisely because we have made the verbal declaration of certain Christian proof-texts and testimonials our focus. This is backward. The power of Jesus is conveyed as God's people LIVE God's principles, not talk about them.

215. You earn the right to be listened to when you speak of spiritual things by the long-lived example of your life.

216. Roots give you the right for your words to be heeded. Personal roots. Maturity. Constancy. Integrity. Living by the Proverbs.

217. God is in the business of permanency, of lifelong principles and truths being infused into character. He takes little interest in disconnected pious words floating out on the air that have His name attached to them.

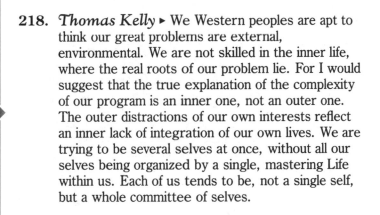

218. *Thomas Kelly* ▸ We Western peoples are apt to think our great problems are external, environmental. We are not skilled in the inner life, where the real roots of our problem lie. For I would suggest that the true explanation of the complexity of our program is an inner one, not an outer one. The outer distractions of our own interests reflect an inner lack of integration of our own lives. We are trying to be several selves at once, without all our selves being organized by a single, mastering Life within us. Each of us tends to be, not a single self, but a whole committee of selves.

219. *Integrate*—To make whole and complete by bringing all the various parts together. Our personal frustrations usually stem from being fractured. Our inner and outer lives are disconnected. Our practical and spiritual lives exist on separate levels. Business and home lives flow on distinctive planes. Therefore, within our inner beings and in our outer relationships there is separation, division, and disunity. God's work all points constantly toward integration.

220. *Frank Laubach* ▸ Two years ago a profound dissatisfaction led me to begin trying to line up my actions with the will of God about every fifteen minutes or half hour. Other people to whom I confessed this intention said it was impossible. But this year I have started out trying to live all my waking moments in conscious listening to the inner voice, asking without ceasing, "What, Father, do you desire said? What, Father, do you desire done this minute?" It is clear that this is exactly what Jesus was doing all day every day. But it is not what His followers have been doing in very large numbers.

221. I was, like Laubach, alone and far from home in a strange land and unfamiliar surroundings, when I discovered him and Kelly and their books. Both men became friends in the spirit. It was not long before I undertook to follow them in their inward quest toward a deeper level of obedience to and communion with the Father. That was twenty-four years ago. My life was never the same afterward. I am looking forward to seeing them in the next life to express my appreciation for such openness in writing about their hearts' joys and struggles. Their words *changed* me.

222. God accomplishes His purposes by planting people with roots, by planting families, by telling them to stay put, and to live as He tells them and to not mix with the world. That's how God operates. Out of the roots thus created, and the lives thus lived, and the separate holy lifestyles thus observed . . . He will miraculously spread His life into all the world. Jesus' Great Commission is a culmination and fulfillment of the foundational principle by which God established the Israelites in the land of promise, not an abolishment of it. God's ways don't change.

223. *George MacDonald* ▸ The highest creation of which man is capable is to will the will of the Father.

224. When we exercise our will, and *choose* to do right, *choose* to obey, *choose* to lay our own personal will aside for that of the Father, then are we vitally acting in the prerogative and power of a son or daughter of God.

225. *George MacDonald* ▸ To obey Jesus is to ascend to the pinnacle of my being.

226. Even Jesus had to discover who His Father was and what His own Sonship meant. Truly, He is our Brother!

227. *George MacDonald* ▸ Any belief *in* Jesus Christ—however small—is far better than any amount of belief *about* him.

228. Seeking and discovering God's Fatherhood is the quest, the journey, the spiritual pilgrimage of life. It is the great story, the essence of history, the very meaning and hidden mysterious thread weaving its way through every human life and every age.

229. *George MacDonald* ▸ He who sits there will not ask, "Did you go to church?" but, "Did you do what I told you?"

230. God wants us to be people of a certain sort, not people who DO certain things. He wants people who reflect the character of His Son.

231. *George MacDonald* ▸ Every fact in nature is a revelation of God.

232. Pruning is necessary for healthy growth and abundance of fruit—for people as well as trees. If given the chance, we will always go away from the light, away from the sky. Read John 15.

233. Keep your spiritual pruning clippers handy—to use on yourself. You have to train the inner streams of your spiritual sap. You have to consciously set the upward direction of the flow inside your trunk or your life will go off in all kinds of random directions.

234. Prune off any motive or influence within you that tries to cause growth in any direction but toward the light. Be self-pruning.

235. *Miles Stanford* ▸ Many of these development areas are just plain desert—no spiritual activity, no service, little or no fellowship with Him, or others. What prayer there is has to be forced and is sometimes dropped altogether for months at a time. Bible study finally grinds to a halt; everything seems to add up to nothing. It is during these necessary times that . . . Our Father strips everything away . . . in order to give us the opportunity of loving and trusting and responding to Him just because He is our Father.

236. It's a good practice to be a morning person, whether you're a morning *or* a night person. Remember Ben Franklin's advice about bedtimes.

237. Schedule your routine tasks ahead. Trying to just fit things in as you find the time is a guaranteed road toward disorganization and inefficiency.

238. *Henry Wadsworth Longfellow* ► It takes less time to do a thing right than to explain why you did it wrong.

239. Plan ahead. Whoever first thought of this was a genius. It never loses its importance.

240. Go into situations and dilemmas asking yourself: How might I do this more efficiently? Is there time to be saved, redundancy to be avoided, energy to be preserved?

241. Efficiency is one of the secret keys to a fulfilled life. It is not a principle reserved for executives, but one of God's most powerful attributes. Read Genesis 1. *Everything* with purpose! Nothing wasted.

242. *William Barclay* ▸ For me the supreme truth of Christianity is that in Jesus I see God. When I see Jesus feeding the hungry, comforting the sorrowing, befriending men and women with whom no one else would have had anything to do, I can say: "This is God."   *A Spiritual Autobiography*

243. What you do, do with passion. What you think, think passionately. What you believe, believe passionately. What you *are, be* passionately. When you obey, obey wholeheartedly.

244. Life is to be *lived,* not muddled through.

245. Above all passions, love truth passionately. Learn to love the 119th Psalm. Be passionate about God's commands, laws, and decrees.

246. *Soren Kierkegaard* ▸ There is always a worldliness that is desirous of having the name of being a Christian but wishes to become one at as cheap a price as possible.   *For Self-Examination*

247. Know the difference between meddling and helping, between an interfering spirit and a spirit of graciousness.

248. *Thomas Kelly* ▸ Meister Eckhart wrote: "There are plenty to follow our Lord half-way, but not the other half. They will give up possessions, friends and honors, but it touches them too closely to disown themselves." It is just this astonishing life which is willing to follow Him the other half, sincerely to disown itself, this life which intends complete obedience, without any reservations, that I would propose to you . . . commit your lives in unreserved obedience to Him. If you don't realize the revolutionary explosiveness of this proposal you don't understand what I mean. Only now and then comes a man or a woman who . . . is willing to be utterly obedient, to go the other half, to follow God's faintest whisper.

249. Being a Christian is a two-step process. Step one is salvation. But one blade of scissors can't do the job. Neither can salvation alone accomplish God's true purpose, which is total personal transformation.

250. The second step, the life of the "second half," being transformed into the image of Jesus, entering into God's full purpose, cannot be done passively. It is an active, daily, strenuous battle to keep self and the motives and priorities and attitudes of self at bay. It cannot be done without prayer and an ongoing communion with God and reliance on His help to accompany our obedience to His commands.

251. *Thomas Kelly* ▸ Once having the vision, the second step to holy obedience is this: Begin where you are. Obey now. Use what little obedience you are capable of, even if it be like a grain of mustard seed. Begin where you are. Live this present moment, this present hour as you now sit in your seat, in utter, utter submission and openness toward Him. Listen outwardly to these words, but within, behind the scenes, in the deeper levels of your lives where you are all alone with God . . . keep up a silent prayer, "Open thou my life. Guide my thoughts . . . Thy will be done."

252. Living in the "Center," living what Kelly calls the "astonishing life of holy obedience," is a death-to-self, put-others-first, interaction-with-God-as-*Lord*-of-every-moment life. Not that you will remember to think of God every second, or even every hour, as Laubach tried to do. I have attempted his "experiment." It is unbelievably difficult! But such a life does mean that your *will* is engaged 24-hours-a-day to do battle against the perspectives of self, the flesh, the old man.

253. The Bible is not a data base from which to accumulate facts and information. It is an instruction manual, the ultimate how-to book . . . the how-to book of life!

254. *George Mueller* ▸ God delights to increase the faith of His children. We ought, instead of wanting no trials before victory, no exercise for patience, to be willing to take them from God's hand as a means. I say—and say it deliberately—trials, obstacles, difficulties, and sometimes defeats, are the very food of faith.   *The Green Letters*

255. Everything reduces to choice.

256. Don't always insist (or even try) on being right. Even if you are, keep it to yourself.

257. *Frank Laubach* ▸ This grey-blue rolling water ringed with whitecaps, hemmed with distant green hills and crowned with colored clouds and baby-blue sky reveals God's love of beauty—and God is so lavish with his paintbrush . . . He is lavish everywhere if one only has eyes to see Him at work.

258. Relish the small things. Look for the mysteries, truths, and revelations of life in the places others don't see. Train yourself to hear the voice of God in the unexpected places.

259. *William Shakespeare* ▸ The earth has music for those who listen.

260. *C. S. Lewis* ▸ The universe rings true wherever you fairly test it. *Surprised by Joy*

261. The truth the universe rings with is nothing less than a picture, a portrait, a portrayal of God's nature and personality. God did not randomly create, nor did He let life randomly evolve. Every inch of the universe resounds with defined purpose. We have to teach ourselves how to see it, how to "fairly test it."

262. *Thomas Kelly* ▸ There is a way of ordering our mental life on more than one level at once. On one level we may be thinking, discussing, seeing, calculating, meeting all the demands of external affairs. But deep within, behind the scenes, at a profounder level, we may also be in prayer. . . . Between the two levels is fruitful interplay, but ever the accent must be on the deeper level, where the soul ever dwells in the presence of the Holy One. For the religious man is forever bringing all affairs of the first level down into the Light, holding them there in the Presence, reseeing them. . . . Facts remain facts, when brought into the Presence in the deeper level, but their value, their significance, is wholly realigned.

263. So many people miss the richness of looking at things on deeper levels. They don't consider the implications and consequences and spiritual dimensions below the surface. Take the road less traveled.

264. Think consequentially and multi-dimensionally.

265. It is sometimes a sign of wisdom to keep quiet and allow people the freedom to make their own mistakes. The immature person always has a word of counsel for everyone. It is the mature person who knows how to guard his words until the moment they will do the most good. Proverbs 12:23.

266. When in doubt whether to offer counsel or advice, wait until you are asked.

267. *Thomas Kelly* ▸ What is here urged are internal practices and habits of the mind. What is here urged are secret habits of unceasing orientation of the deeps of our being about the Inward Light, ways of conducting our inward life so that we are perpetually bowed in worship, while we are also very busy in the world of daily affairs. . . . Yield yourself to Him who is a far better teacher than these outward words, and you will have found the Instructor Himself, of whom these words are a faint and broken echo.

268. I have done as Kelly suggests, attempted to develop "internal practices and habits of the mind" which would "unceasingly orient" my focus toward God in the middle of my day's rigorous affairs. In the attempt I most always feel a failure. Yet it has the effect of revealing to me, as perhaps nothing else can, just what a remarkable life it was that Jesus lived.

269. *George MacDonald* ▸ The refusal, and the inability, to look up to God as our Father is the one central wrong in the whole human affair, the one central misery. Recognizing our Father fully will more or less clear away every difficulty in life.

270. *Ralph Waldo Emerson* ▸ Make the most of yourself, for that is all there is of you.

271. Emerson is so right, yet how little we heed it. I like to rephrase it: Make the most of what God gave you. He gave it so you could fulfill His purpose in it.

272. *George MacDonald* ▸ The one thing the Lord insists upon is the doing of the thing we know we ought to do.

273. Authority proceeds out of a double-sided living within its great covering truth. Only the one who knows how to function "under" authority can properly exercise authority "over" others.

274. *Watchman Nee* ▸ In touching God's authority we touch God Himself. God's work basically is done not by power but by authority. . . . All the laws of the universe are established by God. Everything is under His authority. . . . All Christians must therefore learn to obey authority. . . . Authority is everywhere . . . obedience to authority is the first lesson a worker ought to learn.   *Spiritual Authority*

275. Jesus is the supreme example of living in the fullness of authority. He said that He did *nothing* on His own, but *only* what the Father told Him to do. Therefore, *all* authority has been given Him. It is a principle that lives everywhere in God's kingdom. He lived out His authority by washing the disciples' feet.

276. Authority does not exist without correspondent submission. True authority is rooted in the submission of self-death and in servanthood. Jesus is the clear example of this total unity of submission and authority. Most men and women mistake the nature of both, and therefore function in neither.

277. *C. S. Lewis* ▸ The Christian way is different: harder, and easier. Christ says, "Give me All. I don't want so much of your time and so much of your money and so much of your work: I want You. I have not come to torment your natural self, but to kill it. No half-measures are any good. I don't want to cut off a branch here and a branch there, I want to have the whole tree down. I don't want to drill the tooth, or crown it . . . but to have it out. Hand over the whole natural self, all the desires which you think innocent as well as the ones you think wicked—the whole outfit. I will give you a new self instead. In fact, I will give you Myself: my own will shall become yours.

278. *Francis Schaeffer* ▸ There is only one reason to believe in Christianity. Because it is true.

279. Never allow truth to be abstract.

280. There is only one verse in the Bible that succinctly gives us the essence of God's being by telling us what He IS. His character *contains* justice and power and judgment and many other qualities we do well to fear. But what He **IS** in a word . . . is love.

281. *C. S. Lewis* ▸ Every time you make a choice you are turning the central part of you, the part of you that chooses, into something a little different from what it was before. And taking your life as a whole, with all your innumerable choices, all your life long you are slowly turning this central thing into a heavenly creature or into a hellish creature.

282. *George MacDonald* ▸ There is no teacher like obedience, and no obstruction like its postponement.

283. Don't mistake what is the *real* "you." You can call it whatever you want—your heart, your mind, your soul, your self, your inner being. But the *real*est, *central*est, *deep*est place that is just you and you alone, where not even God himself can go—that is your *will*. God gave it to you to be absolutely and completely yours. You don't even have to share it with Him! It's the place within you that makes choices and decisions. How you make use of that private little place determines what kind of person you become, and what the *real* YOU is like.

284. Most have not learned to discipline their wills. They follow desire instead. But will can function even in the midst of the ups and downs of fleeting desires and feelings. You command yourself into action through willpower as *you* choose, no matter what emotions are present or absent. When you command your will, you direct your course.

285. The *will* is the boiler room of the mind and heart and total being. The will is where power is generated and where accomplishment and growth begin. Its vast resources are harnessed and set in motion by a singular act we must carry out—the act of *decision*. Decision is the on-switch. It engages the entire dynamic process.

286. Your will changes every time you make a decision. With every choice *toward self,* it becomes more strongly oriented toward self. With every choice away from self and *toward self-denial,* it becomes stronger in the direction of Christlikeness. Your decisions change you a tiny bit every day, as your will becomes stronger or weaker in the direction you have set yourself to go.

287. Obey Scripture first, then try to understand its deeper nuances later. Never wait to obey until after you understand completely.

288. *Oswald Chambers* ▸ We are not to be numbskulls, but holy men, full-blooded and holy to the last degree, not anemic creatures without enough strength to be bad. The relation to life ordained by Jesus Christ does not unsex men and women but enables them to be holy men and women. *Still Higher for His Highest*

289. Never flirt—with the opposite sex, the world's value structure, or the devil's methods. It's a dangerous game.

290. If you find yourself in the presence of one flirting with any of the above, seek different company immediately. If you hang around, you can be assured they will make every effort to subtly draw you in.

291. Pray for holiness to be infused into and then reflected out of your being and character.

292. Goodness alone won't get you into heaven. But goodness *is* a good thing. Jesus told us to be good. Therefore . . . be a good person.

293. *Judy Phillips* ▸ God looks over His world, then bends down and picks up our broken pieces. They have value to Him, not because He will put them back together, but because He will transform them into precious stones.—(An anniversary memory, after twenty years with one I love . . . a very *good thing to remember.* But only for me.)

294. Demonstrate giving, sacrificial kindness to those with whom you live and work every day.

295. *Anonymous* ▸ There are only two lasting bequests you can give your children. One is roots, the other wings.

296. Don't be in a hurry for your children to become grown. The longer you can stretch out their childhood and youth, the more solid will be their adulthood. Roots need time to fully develop.

297. Any man can be a father. But it takes someone special, with lots of dedication and sacrifice, to be a dad.

298. Don't leave your children a fortune. It's one of the most crippling legacies you could pass on to them. Give them your character instead.

299. *Anonymous* ▸ Do not pray for an easy life. Pray to be a strong person.

300. Have two or three favorite Bible translations. It will help keep you open-minded, as well as more knowledgeable in the Scriptures.

301. Refuse to assert yourself in the way of worldly recognition and gain.

302. *Henry Drummond* ▸ There is a great difference between *trying to please* and *giving pleasure*. Give pleasure. Lose no chance of giving pleasure. For that is the ceaseless and anonymous triumph of a truly loving spirit. "I shall pass through this world but once. Any good thing therefore that I can do, or any kindness that I can show to any human being, let me do it now. Let me not defer it or neglect it, for I shall not pass this way again."

303. Give pleasure to those you meet first with your mouth. No one can resist a bright smile! Flash your teeth and watch the response—a smile will nearly always greet you back in return! Let the pleasure-giving spread to your eyes. Then let your whole face widen in greeting as you speak a kind and gracious word. You will, with such a simple expenditure of energy, have given pleasure, and thus furthered the kingdom of God.

304. *Watchman Nee* ▸ Man's action should not be governed by the knowledge of good or evil; it should be motivated by a sense of obedience. . . . Countless Christians are living today in a state of rebellion; they have not so much as learned the first lesson in obedience. . . . As faith is the principle by which we obtain life, so obedience is the principle by which that life is lived out. *Spiritual Authority*

305. *George MacDonald* ▸ Men must understand that neither thought nor talk, neither sorrow for sin nor love of holiness is required of them, but obedience. To *be* and *obey* are one.

306. Modernistic thinking is rooted in the assumptions that: (1) We don't have to do anything except what is *right*; (2) *We* have the "right" to determine what *right* is for ourselves. Christians who eagerly follow this line of thinking need to be warned: Both assumptions are dead wrong!

307. True *life* lies in obedience to a higher standard than our own self-motivated determinations of supposed "right." It involves a higher standard even than right and wrong itself. We are to obey God's authority . . . God himself. In such obedience is life and freedom indeed!

308. Think of commands and instructions and teachings as "light," and as the way to life, not as constrictions upon your freedom. Eagerly hunger to be instructed.

309. *Henry Drummond* ▸ Where Love is, God is. He that dwelleth in Love dwelleth in God. God is Love. Therefore *love*. Without distinction, without calculation, without procrastination, love. Lavish it upon the poor, where it is very easy; especially upon the rich, who often need it most; most of all upon our equals, where it is very difficult, and for whom perhaps we each do least of all.

310. The old code of the West is still a pretty good thing to remember. Be a man or woman of your honor . . . of your word.

311. Whole sub-theologies are built around tiny portions of scripture that are singularly well-suited for externalization. That's what the sects of Jesus' day were based on, and evangelicals have a wide range of mini-sects among them today. Find and live by the *larger* truths, not the tiny ones.

312. *George MacDonald* ▸ O Lord, let my faults by thy hand be corrected.

313. Prayerful self-introspection according to the principles of Psalm 51 and 139 is not to be reserved only for contemplative mystics. It's an integral aspect of one's inner growth.

314. *Johann Wolfgang von Goethe* ▸ Knowing is not enough; we must apply. Willing is not enough; we must do.

315. Like David, we are to invite the probing light of the Spirit into the innermost hidden chambers of our being, to shine upon the dark places and cleanse them out of us.

316. Keep your perspective on Scripture large, encompassing, balanced. Wherever you find a passage upon which it seems reasonable to base a conclusion, try to find another passage that seems to indicate a *different* perspective. It's a good exercise to keep you open to the fact that the Bible doesn't give us many proof-texts to verify dogmatism. There are very often seeming contradictions in it. Then go to the Father and ask *Him* to show you truth. The Bible is to point to Him, not be a substitute.

317. *Frank Laubach* ▸ This has been a week of wonders. God is at work *everywhere* . . . I have discovered . . . that it is a continuous discovery. Every day is rich with new aspects of Him and His working.

318. Value your roots. We all have them extending in multiple directions—family roots, spiritual roots, old friends, even memories and places and experiences, books and periods of growth. Everything we've experienced goes into the substrata of the soil from which we are nurtured into maturity.

319. *George MacDonald* ▸ We do not understand the *next* page of God's lesson book; we see only the one before us. When we understand the one before us, only then are we able to turn the next.

320. Remain open to all, yet be selective in committing yourself to relationship. Be friendly and gracious, yet careful in commitments. *Everyone* will rub off on you. Make sure the influences are good ones.

321. *Miles Stanford* ▸ Most of our true spiritual development comes through the dry and hard times.

322. Find something to like in every kind of weather. What purpose does it serve? Look forward with anticipation to changes. Such an outlook will keep all times of the year new and full of zest. Apply this principle not only to the weather. Find something to like in *every* circumstance.

323. *William Barclay* ▸ I have an essentially second-class mind . . . but I can sit down and work. I don't make the slightest claim to inspiration in preaching or writing. I only claim to have gone to work as any working man must go.   *A Spiritual Autobiography*

324. What an example! The man wrote 50 or 75 books and is one of the great disseminators of biblical truth in this century, yet he traces his impact back to mere obedience, to doing what God placed before him, to plain old hard work. I've benefitted from many of those books and Barclay's practical and loving approach to Scripture. But even above his ideas, the life-example of steadfastness and faithfulness shines through. How greatly we can all learn from him!

325. When we do what God gives us to do, He *will* use it for His purposes.

326. *George MacDonald* ▸ To the foundation of yesterday's work well done, the work of tomorrow will be sure to fit. Work *done* is of more consequence for the future than all the foresight and planning of an archangel.

327. It's generally of little value to take notes of sermons. Respond with your heart, not your brain. Let obedience follow, not analysis.

328. *Mr. Fred Rogers* ▸ There's no one in the whole world just like you.

329. Never envy another. God has endowed everyone with talents, but yours are unlike anyone else's.

330. *Henry David Thoreau* ▸ If a man does not keep pace with his companions, perhaps it is because he hears a different drummer. Let him step to the music he hears, however measured or far away.

331. Nonconformity for the purpose of making life annoying to those around you is hardly a virtue. Nonconformity because you're trying to obey Romans 12:2 is one of the primary avenues by which God intends to take the gospel throughout the world.

332. *Miles Stanford* ▸ One of God's most effective means in the process is failure . . . the main instrument in the Father's hand for conforming us to the image of his Son.

333. Personal integrated wholeness is one component of a life well-lived in the truths of God. Everything lines up. All life's pieces fit into a unity. The outer is a reflection of the inner. Trinitarian *Three-ness* is visible—wholeness . . . integration. Pray for your Father to accomplish this purpose in your life!

"Three-ness"

The number three signifies completeness. In *threes* has God ordained to reveal himself to His creation and to mankind—his *own* distinct kind within it.

God's own character is comprised of *three* distinct personalities, all pointing to His singleness of being:

(1) The Father, without whom there could be no passing on of life to sons and daughters.

(2) The Son, without whom there could be no "fatherhood."

(3) The Holy Spirit, without whom the "spirit" of life could not be transmitted.

God uniquely created the family as a threefold unit to reflect these *three* images or representatives of His being:

(1) Fathers are to portray aspects of God's Fatherhood.

(2) Mothers are to portray aspects of the working of the Holy Spirit.

(3) Children are to exemplify in their relationships with their parents Jesus' own trusting relationship to His heavenly Father.

The task of God's people is to spend their lives engaged in *three* callings which represent the sum total of a human being's purpose and destiny on earth:

(1) To *discover* and intimately *know* the character and nature of God's Fatherhood.

(2) To *live* moment by moment in the "sonship" relation to that Fatherhood.

(3) To *pass on* to others (your own sons and daughters as well as all those with whom you have to do) the truths and principles of that Fatherhood.

In the number **333**, therefore, we have a constant reminder of God's being, the family, and our call as God's men and women, sons and daughters, to live in the fullness of his Fatherhood.

GOOD THINGS TO REMEMBER

Good Things To Remember

Good Things To Remember

Good Things To Remember

GOOD THINGS TO REMEMBER

Good Things To Remember

GOOD THINGS TO REMEMBER

Credits

Unless noted otherwise, quotations from the following authors are from these books:

C. S. Lewis: *Mere Christianity,* 1952, The Macmillan Co.
Thomas Kelly: *A Testament of Devotion,* 1941, Harper & Row
Frank Laubach: *Letters by a Modern Mystic,* 1937, Fleming H. Revell
George MacDonald: *Discovering the Character of God,* 1989, Bethany House Publishers and *Knowing the Heart of God,* 1990, Bethany House Publishers
Henry Drummond: *The Greatest Thing in the World,* Fleming H. Revell
Miles Stanford: *The Green Letters,* 1972, Back to the Bible Broadcast